# TRENTHAM

## HISTORY TOUR

# ACKNOWLEDGEMENTS

My thanks must go to Newcastle-under-Lyme Library, Stoke-on-Trent City Archives and Keele University for their unfailing patience when presented with complicated requests. Thanks to Miss Barbara Fieldhouse, a sweet ninety-year-old lady who is a family friend of the Scott family and helped to fill in the gaps whilst making a smashing cup of tea in proper china cups. Thanks also to film actress Janette Scott for generously sharing family photographs and relating stories of her time spent in Trentham. Thanks to Dave Cooke who is always willing to help. Final thanks must go to my loving wife Glynis who always helps and supports me in everything I attempt, even when the task seems impossible.

First published 2019

Amberley Publishing
The Hill, Stroud,
Gloucestershire, GL5 4EP
www.amberley-books.com

Copyright © Alan Myatt, 2019
Map contains Ordnance Survey data
© Crown copyright and database
right [2019]

The right of Alan Myatt to be identified as the Author of this work has been asserted in accordance with the Copyrights, Designs and Patents Act 1988.

British Library Cataloguing in Publication Data.
A catalogue record for this book is available from the British Library.

ISBN 978 1 4456 5213 9 (print)
ISBN 978 1 4456 5214 6 (ebook)

Origination by Amberley Publishing.
Printed in Great Britain.

# INTRODUCTION

Planning the route of a history tour around Trentham proved quite a challenge. Unlike the tour of a town, Trentham has no centre around which to navigate; it is spread over a wide area and requires lots of legwork to cover the chosen route of around 8 miles. Another problem is the timescale. Trentham's pedigree goes back 2,000 years or more and it would be impossible to include everything. Therefore, I have chosen a period of around 200 years to explore.

The route covers newly created farms and parkland, which has since disappeared beneath modern-day of life. The explosion in population caused huge problems for the dukes of Sutherland. The duke fought hard against the ever-growing tide of effluent that flowed from the streets that he had created to house the people who worked in mines and workshops. The solution was beyond his capabilities alone and the results of involving the authorities will be visited.

There are many people who have interesting life stories but that would fill a volume on its own, so instead I have selected a handful of Trentham residents who I thought might interest the reader. One story that has always intrigued me is the one about film actress Janette Scott having family in Trentham. This remained in my mind after she visited Heron Cross School in 1957 when I was a pupil. I was lucky enough to be able to contact Janette who kindly supplied family stories and photos, finally allowing me to gather the facts after sixty years of wondering. So dear reader, enjoy the tour.

# 1. BLURTON WASTE FARM

Blurton Waste Farm was built in 1811, created out of several outlying portions of other farms. The first tenant, Mr John Townsend, descended from one of the oldest families in Trentham, his ancestors having tenanted land under Lord Stafford for nearly 200 years. An allowance of lime was given provided he purchased a large quantity of manure from Longton. The duke leased 252 acres of waste farm to the corporation for a sewage farm in 1894.

# 2. HEM HEATH COLLIERY

The first sod was cut in July 1924 by the 5th Duke of Sutherland on part of Blurton Waste Farm called Gorsty Hill. The number one shaft was 19 feet in diameter. Newstead Brook had to be diverted to the perimeter of the site. A chimney 180 feet high was built, and number two shaft was sunk in 1950 with the landmark 'A' frame that was a favourite roost for hundreds of starlings. It was demolished in the early morning of 19 August 1977 by NCB in fear of it being listed.

Staffordshire Wildlife Trust

Welcome to

# Hem Heath Wood

# 3. HEM HEATH WOODS

Burnt Heath was enclosed in 1752 by Lord Gower, who desired a new park to complement the one at Trentham. The canal cut came through in 1771, isolating a corner of the parkland. Around 1784 the idea was abandoned and it became New Park Farm; John Mills was the first tenant. In 1847 a railway divided the farm in half and in 1851 the portion to the east was made a plantation, with a commemorative stone inscribed with the date. This is still there today.

# 4. TRENTHAM STATION

The North Staffordshire Railway intended to build a level crossing across Longton Road but the duke insisted on a bridge. He also insisted on a station to allow the Ducal family and guests easy access to Trentham Hall, with signals to stop the trains. It was designed by Charles Barry to complement Trentham Hall style and was completed 1851. Fresh flowers were dispatched daily for Stafford House, London. Many noble feet paraded the platform here.

# 5. KING GEORGE V BLIND HOME AND SELWYN HOUSE

'Selwyn' was home to Alfred Corn, director of Richards Tiles, until his death in 1916 aged fifty. His brother Edmund lived there until 1936 when he gifted the house to the blind welfare committee to be used

as a blind home for twelve persons to be named in honour of the late king. Arthur Critchlow of Blurton Post Office was there in 1936. He had one glass eye and worked at Blurton Tilery. The house was replaced with 'Selwyn House' nursing home.

# 6. MASTER BUILDER

William Mould built many houses in Trentham and lived at 'Sunnyside', which he constructed. Born in 1865 at the Royal Oak pub in Fenton, his father Francis was the landlord. Large portions of Hem Heath were sold off in 1896 and Mould took advantage. He constructed fifty-two houses. 'Sunnyside', No. 265, was three doors away from Trentham station. He died on 15 June 1949 aged eighty-five, and is buried at Trentham with his wife Amy who died earlier that year.

# 7. CHIEF CONSTABLE BUNN

Frank Leonard Bunn was chief constable of eight separate police forces, a record that can't be broken because many have disappeared. Born in Norfolk in 1890 and arriving in Stoke-on-Trent in 1936, he initiated the use of two-way radio. His official residence was Heath House, No. 219 Longton Road. A house fire next door took the life of an overweight gentleman – his body was welded to the floorboards by body fat. Constable Alf Botfield was surprised his superior was not alerted by the smell. Bunn died in 1974 in Cambridge.

# 8. TRENTHAM HOTEL

The Roebuck Inn, beside the canal, was destroyed by fire in 1865. A new Trentham Hotel was built nearby, opening in 1868. It had a large bowling green at the rear and a menagerie. In the 1930s several monkeys escaped when a cage door was left open, causing chaos in the village. One conceited individual was found sitting on a dressing table in a house on Barlaston Road admiring himself in a hand mirror. The hotel is now a Toby Carvery.

# 9. HEM HEATH SMITHY

The Blacksmiths and Wheelwrights was built in 1823 to service the traffic on the highway and canal wharf next door. It had 8 acres of land, which was farmed. In modern times Thompsons Coach Tours had a depot at the rear.

They sold out to Copelands in 1985 after several vehicles were torched during the miners' strike, in the mistaken belief that they were bussing strike breakers. They were in fact giving free day trips to miners' families.

# 10. NEW PARK

The farmhouse was taken over by George Cooper with 48 acres in 1849. It was then owned by solicitor Thomas Llewellyn, who farmed as a sideline. Another solicitor, Samuel Cooper from Newcastle, was his successor. His wife refused entry to the duke's mistress, Mary Blair, when the duke knocked on the door whilst riding. Cooper was given notice the next day. John Bailey, manager of Doulton's, took over until 1936, followed by Joseph Tellwright, colliery owner, in 1940, who rebuilt it. He died in 1966 and it became a teacher's retirement home. It is now a nursing home owned by Bill Morris, co-owner of The Place nightclub at Hanley.

# 11. LIMEKILN BRIDGE

From New Park, Jonathon Road leads to Lime Kiln Bridge, No. 105 on the Trent and Mersey Canal. This was the western entrance to New Park Farm.

Limestone was carried down the Cauldon Canal from Cauldon Quarry and loaded into the top of the kiln and heated to make quicklime, which was spread on the land to boost crop production. There are stories of workmen and horses falling into other kilns and being roasted to death. Just the bridge remains today.

# 12. SEWAGE WORKS

Continue to Barlaston Road and Strongford Sewage Works is encountered.

Blurton Sewage Farm proved inadequate and a new drain connecting it to Strongford was laid in 1951. The water quality is so good after purification that visitors are given a glass to drink, with no ill effects. The sludge from the works was taken in tankers and sprayed onto old slag heaps to aid growth.

Fish are now returning to the River Trent beside the sewage works.

# 13. METHODIST CHAPEL

The Wesleyan Methodist Chapel was designed by the estate surveyor Thomas Roberts, on the first plot of land leased from Trentham. The cost of building was £500. One minister named Richard Webb was born in Penzance and his first ministry was the Shetland Isles. Subsequently he preached at Banff, Daventry, Glamorgan, Berkshire, and finally Trentham. He died in 1912 and is buried in Trentham Cemetery. Completed in 1883, the chapel contains some early Doulton tiles by George Tinworth.

# 14. GOLF CLUB

The golf course opened in 1894. The first president was Revd Edmund Pigott. Duchess Millicent was keen to establish a ladies' golf club and helped replace the wooden pavilion of 1896 with the present clubhouse which opened in 1904. It was designed as a private house in case the golf course was not a success – then it could be sold off. Unfortunately, a public footpath runs across the green from Ash Green roundabout to Barlaston Old Road.

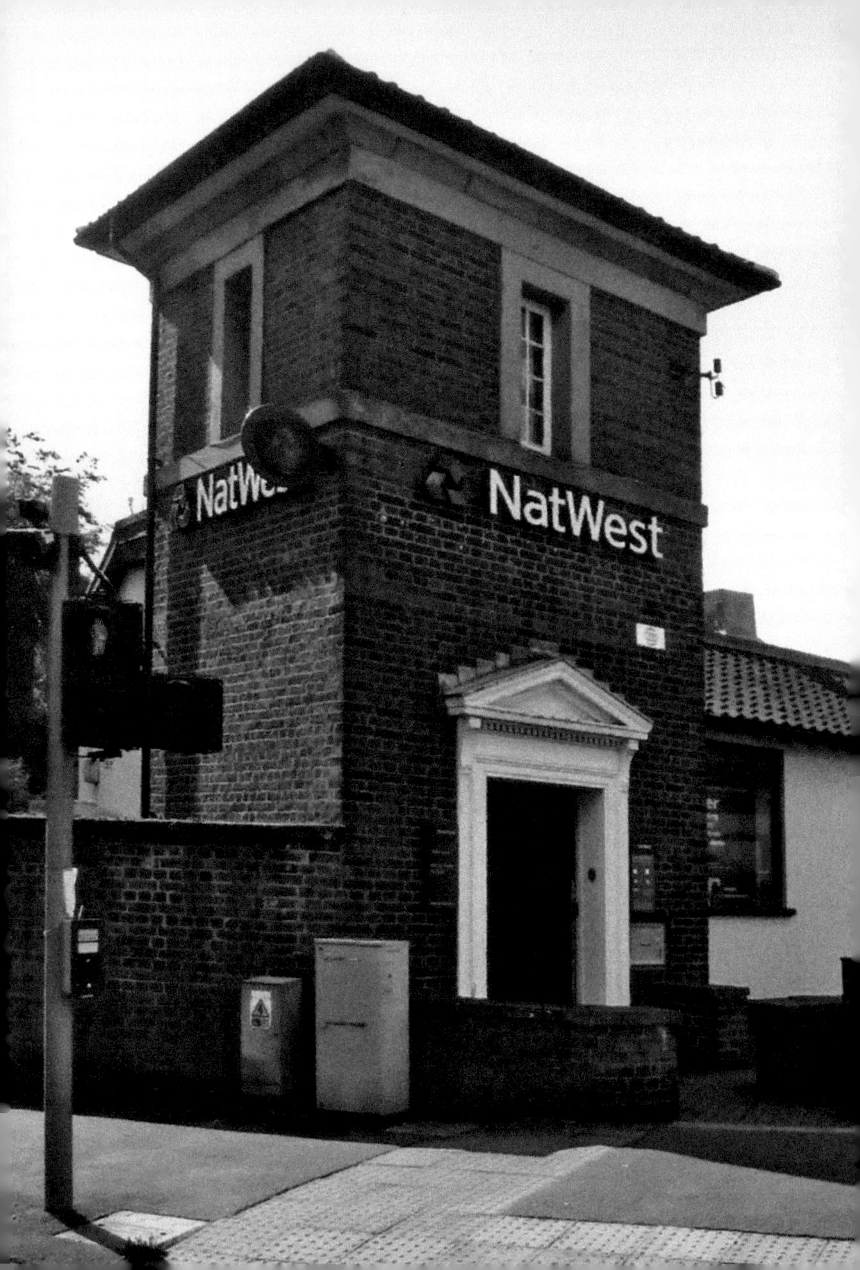
NatWest
NatWest

# 15. OLD POLICE STATION

Trentham Police Station was designed by Charles Barry in 1843.

It cost the Duke of Sutherland £280 to build and he rented it to the authorities at £16 per year. It had accommodation for four officers.

The site was chosen as a consequence of the recent Potteries Riots, when a mob had planned to march on Trentham Hall. A small tower on the roof was used for messenger pigeons to share intelligence with other police stations.

# 16. ABRAHAM FIELDING

Simon Fielding leased a plot of land next to the police station in 1887 where he built his house. His son Abraham leased two more next door in 1894 and built two substantial houses for himself and his brother-in-law, with 'A. F. and J. T. 1894' inscribed on the gable ends. Abraham took over the Railway Pottery, which his father had invested in, changing its name to Crown Devon in Wheildon Road, Stoke, which became very successful.

TRENTHAM

TRENTHAM ½
STONE 5½
STAFFORD 12½

LONGTON 3½

# 17. MILEPOST

Facing New Inn Lane stands a survivor of the coaching age. Longton Road was turnpiked in 1771, and by law mileposts had to be erected. Many got damaged or lost, and in 1893 Charles Latham of Tipton received an order for 335 triangular cast-iron replacements. Most of these were scrapped during road-widening schemes. Only two survive on this road; the other is at Newstead Industrial Estate, facing Tilery Lane.

## 18. TRENTHAM GARAGE

Opposite the milepost is a knoll that was once a triangular green. The road to the west was blocked up and built on. The garage photograph was taken in 1953 when it was owned by Townsends. During building work involving new foundations for an extension in 1973, two human skeletons were unearthed. The coroner pronounced them to be ancient. It is likely they were executed murderers or suicides, as they were always buried at crossroads to confuse the troubled spirits.

TRENTHAM GAR
LONGTON ROAD
PHO

E (PROP. W.A.TOWNSEND)

RENTHAM S:O.-T.

49065

# 19. NEW INN LANE

This ancient lane was the continuation of Barlaston Road, which was falling out of use by 1622 due to constant flooding. A new inn was built by the mid-1700s named The Bulls Head, which gave New Inn Lane its name. New Inn Mill (Brassingtons) was leased to Richard Foley, ironmaster of Longton, in 1669 as a corn mill. It then become Obidiah Lane, nameed for the gentleman who lived at Longton Hall and was lord of the manor. The leet to the waterwheel was cut from Longton Brook and passed beneath the building.

# 20. MAN IN SPACE

The Man in Space pub was opened on 12 April 1961, named in honour of the first man in space, Russian cosmonaut Yuri Gagarin. There are only three pubs in the country with that name including one at Stockwell near Bristol and another at Eastwood, Notts, which featured briefly in the film *Carry on at Your Convenience*, and which was demolished in 2011. Gagarin, who was a mere 5 feet 2 inches tall, died in a fighter plane crash in 1968. His ashes are buried in Red Square behind Lenin's tomb.

# 21. JANETTE SCOTT AND THORA HIRD'S GOLDEN WEDDING

Film star Janette Scott used to spend the long summer school holidays with her Auntie Reet at No. 15 Highfield Avenue, Trentham. Harriet Rita Scott was born in 1912. Her father, James, was a cellist at the Theatre Royal, Hanley, and also conducted the orchestra at Stoke Hippodrome. Rita became a schoolteacher at Stoke Saint Peters, then headmistress at Glass Street School, Hanley. She was offered the headship of Birches Head High School and worked closely with the architects on its design. She moved to a bungalow in Trentley Road and retired to live in a flat at Stone in 1979, where she suffered a stroke and died in hospital in 2000. Janette Scott is at the front of the image, with Auntie Reet on the right. Thora Hird and Jimmy Scott are with James Torme, Daisy Torme and William Rademaeker, Janett's children and husband.

# 22. TURBINE GARAGE AND THE SLUICE GATES

The Duke of Sutherland employed a Stoke contractor named Frederick Barke to construct a dam on the River Trent with a channel to feed two turbine generators that were to be installed in an old corn mill in 1894. Sharpe & Kent fitted the generators at a cost of £983, 9s 11d, including cable to Trentham Hall and electrical fittings there. The task was completed in just twelve months. Unfortunately, the hall was demolished eighteen years later.

The generator pits were discovered when inspection pits were being dug at Hisseys Garage.

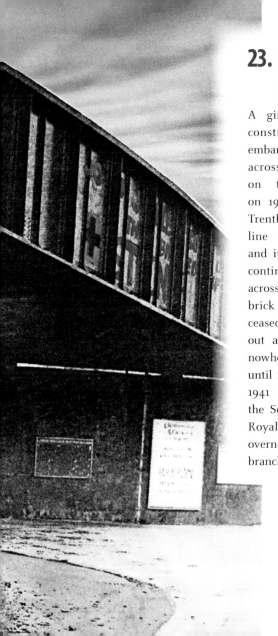

## 23. BRIDGE TO NOWHERE

A girder bridge was constructed on the embankment and rolled across the highway on timber supports on 19 September 1914. Trentham Park branch line opened in 1910 and it was intended to continue to Newcastle across the floodplain on brick arches. Building ceased when war broke out and the bridge to nowhere stood in limbo until it was removed in 1941 for scrap during the Second World War. Royal trains parked overnight on this quiet branch line.

## 24. MAUSOLEUM

The mausoleum was designed by Charles Heathcote Tatham and completed in 1808 at a cost of £5,068 12s. The mausoleum was vital because the Leveson-Gower vault in the church was full with the burial of Lady Susan in 1805. Over 760 Hollington Stone blocks are visible, the largest, beneath the window, weighs over 2 tons. Twenty-nine massive stone slabs form the 40-foot-square base, resting on house bricks. The mausoleum is also 40 feet in height.

# 25. BENCHMARK

Benchmarks are indicated on Ordnance Survey maps by 'B.M'. The arrow points to a line or bronze bolt which is the height above sea level at Newlyn at that point. This one on the mausoleum boundary wall does not appear on the maps. There were other benchmarks on the bridge over Longton Brook a few yards away, and River Trent Bridge on Whitmore Road. Several others disappeared during road widening, along with the mileposts.

# 26. WAR MEMORIAL

Trentham war memorial was unveiled on 2 October 1921 by Colonel Sir Smith Hill-Child. It is made of Darley Dale stone and inscribed with seventeen names of casualties. One name is missing: Benjamin Lincoln Warrington, aged twenty-four, who was blown to pieces on the attack on Cambria on 30 May 1917. He was a shepherd on his father's farm at Butterton Grange. His father, Sampson, moved to Penkridge but is buried at Trentham. His son Benjamin is remembered on the gravestone.

1914 — IN — 1918
GRATEFUL MEMORY
OF THE
MEN OF TRENTHAM
WHO FELL
IN THE GREAT WAR

JOSEPH BASSETT
WILLIAM EDWARD BRAMWICK
WILLIAM CLARKE
WILLIAM CHALLINER
CLAUDE CARLOW FORBE
STANLEY FROLER
ALLAN STUART HUCHES
THOMAS HENDRICK
STEVEN CHARLES JONES
LEONARD JOHNSON
WILLIAM JONES
GEORGE WILLIAM PAGET

# 27. ENTRANCE LODGES

Opposite are two limestone entrance lodges built in 1803 by Charles Heathcote Tatham, large enough to contain one room. They were designed to guard the west entrance of Trentham Hall in the park. A buck and doe deer surmounted the apex. It was moved to its present site when Trentham Gardens Ltd was established, and a public entrance made on what was originally the private drive used by the noble family to convey bodies to the mausoleum across the highway.

# 28. HARVESTER PUB AND CAFÉ MONICA

Harvester was opened as The Poachers Cottage pub in 1975. It was an old estate cottage that escaped demolition when the village was remodeled in the 1840s. Arthur Shenton from Tean converted it to tearooms and a shop in 1921 but died the following year. His widow continued the business, which became Café Monica. It had silver service waitresses in 'Lyons Nippy' uniforms and white linen tablecloths. It even had its own crockery emblazoned with 'Café Monica', made up the road in Longton.

# CAFÉ MONICA

## *for*

## LIGHT LUNCHEONS
## AND DAINTY TEAS
### AT VERY MODERATE PRICES

*Only the Purest of Foods used*

**COMFORT AND CLEANLINESS A SPECIALITY**

## TRENTHAM, Stoke-on-Trent

# 29. OLD SCHOOL

Charles Barry designed the four cottages on Park Drive built in 1842 as eye-catchers to visitors approaching the hall. They were built on the site of earlier dwellings. Robert Wright, brewer and baker, John Macbeth, Scottish Piper, and stud groom Richard Topping were the first occupants. The middle cottage was a Sunday school but was later used as a girls' school to replace the Duchess's School at the other end of Park Drive facing the kennels.

# 30. THE SAWMILL

The villagers of Trentham were alarmed on the night of Saturday 6 October 1894 by the violent ringing of the hall bell. A fire had broken out at the rear of Home Farm in the sawmill. The flames could be seen all over the village as they lit the night sky. All the machinery was destroyed and the carpenters shop seemed doomed. The cost of replacement was £1,000, covered by insurance. The fact that the fire engine was stored in the same yard did not help.

# 31. PEACOCK HOUSE

The poulters' house was built after the completion of the hall, with a tall tower incorporating the entwined double 'S' of the Sutherlands. Simon Fielding was an authority on dogs and poultry and was employed to provide a plentiful supply of birds and fresh eggs for the hall kitchens. He also bred show birds and was a judge at many competitions. He invested in the Railway Pottery at Fenton but his son Abraham had to rescue the venture.

## 32. GAS HOUSE

Opposite is an old quarry used during the building of Trentham Hall, the perfect place to construct a gasometer to store coal gas away from other buildings for fear of explosion. The gas was produced by specialist Elijah Derbyshire from Worsley in Lancashire, where the duke's brother Lord Francis resided. Elijah produced gas for thirty-five years before being asked to relocate to Dunrobin where the duke had built another new gasworks. Elijah died in 1906.

# 33. ICEHOUSE

In the quarry face behind the gas house is a small entrance cut into the rock with a downward-leading passage that emerges into a bottle oven-shaped cavern lined with house bricks. This was the new icehouse built in 1840 to replace an earlier one beside Trentham lake, from where ice was collected during winter to preserve meat, insulated with straw. One has to wonder why, with plenty of venison in the park?

## 34. DUCHESS'S SCHOOL

On the corner of Park Drive is a pair of Georgian cottages that escaped demolition during remodeling of the village. The Duchess of Sutherland had one converted into a girls' school and the other became the school headmistress, Mary Harris's, house. The school had thirty-five pupils who were fitted out with uniforms. Allowances were made for 1 pint of milk per day, 1 peck of potatoes per week and, surprisingly, 1 quart of beer a day.

SWYNNERTON PARISH COUNCIL NOTICES

## 35. PILGRIMS WAY

Just around the corner was an ancient footpath used by pilgrims travelling from St Chad's shrine at Lichfield to St Werburgh's at Chester. They always carried a staff to test the depth of water-filled potholes and fight off wild dogs or robbers. They also carried a scrip bag containing a scallop shell, which was the sign of a pilgrim. The path proceeded through Audlem to Chester, and has only recently disappeared beneath a metal cabinet.

**15**

Parkway

# 36. THE HUNT KENNELS

The Marquis of Stafford was a breeder of Alpine mastiff and spaniel dogs.

He asked his father's permission to build kennels on spare ground beside the River Trent to indulge his interest in breeding hunting dogs. When the 2nd Duke returned from his travels he was surprised at the scale and progress of the new kennels. Designed by Charles Barry, they became the home of the North Staffordshire Hunt in 1863.

# 37. PARK GATES

Entering the park gates you will notice two stone piers in the hedgerow. These are the last vestiges of the Trentham Hall built by William Smith of Warwick in 1710. The associated railings are also by Smith. The cast-iron inner piers are by Walter Macfarlane and Co. of Saracen Lane, Gallowgate, Glasgow (1817–85). An astonishing amount of his work was requisitioned during the Second World War, with possibly the missing gates.

# 38. DAIRY HOUSE

The Dairy House was used by Major Hugh Fraser during his election campaign of 1945. Accompanying him was a young American newspaper reporter named John Fitzgerald Kennedy, who was asked to report on how the British system worked. Kennedy attended Broadway Cinema, Meir, to hear his speech. Fraser became MP for Stone until his death from lung cancer in 1984.

Kennedy became president and his daughter was seeing Mark Shand, brother of Camilla Parker-Bowles, who broke her heart by dumping her.

# 39 AND 40. MILITARY CAMP REMAINS

Across the valley are the remains of a military camp slowly being devoured by vegetation. The French Foreign Legion was the most exotic occupant, evacuated from Norway. Barbara Powner, born in 1925, remembers their officers, with ankle-length cloaks, inspecting Blurton House near her home for officers' quarters.

They found it unsuitable and it was used to store tinned food during the war instead. Just the hut foundations remain in the woods today.

The West Entrance, Trentham Gardens.

# 41. PORTE COCHERE

Through the perimeter fence of Trentham Estate the Porte Cochère can be seen, which was the main entrance to Trentham Hall. The two limestone lodges that flanked it were removed to Stone Road facing the mausoleum.

To the right of the Porte Cochère was the private conservatory and family apartments overlooking the lake and gardens. To the left were the guest bedrooms and the grand staircase. The 2nd Duke of Sutherland's arms sit proudly over the entrance.

# Old Trentham Church.
Tower demolished 1762. Rebuilt 1842.

# 42. ST MARY'S CHURCH

The nave of Trentham Priory Church was not demolished because it was also the parish church. By 1752 the tower had become unstable and was taken down. The bells were sold to Wolstanton in 1767 as it seemed unlikely a new tower would be built. The church was becoming dilapidated also and did not sit well with the new Trentham Hall, so it was rebuilt in 1844. The Norman pillars were carefully numbered and rebuilt in their original position from centuries ago.

# 43. STABLE YARD

Next to the church is the stable yard. In the centre was another building, which has since been removed. The missing building had more stables and accommodation above for the stable lads. This presented a problem as the stable hands fraternised with the dairy maids in the dairy below the clock tower. A new dairy was built in the park to reduce the dalliances, and confusingly it was called 'The Old Dairy House' and was used by the Sutherlands when they visited in later years.

## 44 AND 45. BALLROOM

Trentham Gardens Ltd needed to attract more visitors and decided to build an entertainment hall. It was designed by Stanley Drew of London and financed by the sale of a painting by Romney titled *Countess of Sutherland.*

It opened 1931 with a polished Maplewood dance floor covering 18,000 feet.

Dancing was to a new Panatrope which played vinyl records, later replaced by dance bands that became famous throughout the Midlands. The ballroom was demolished in 2002, becoming the Blue Diamond Shopping Hall.

# 46. TRENTHAM LAKE

Originally this area was marshland and not very inviting. In 1697 a long causeway was constructed running south with a canal on either side, fed by a stream from Kings Wood. Dog racing took place along the causeway. In 1733 the west canal was reshaped with a serpentine edge to make it more natural. The causeway was removed in 1747, creating a 50-acre lake, doubled in size by Capability Brown. The River Trent diverted into it.

# 47. THE MONUMENT

James Loch proposed building monuments at Trentham, Lilleshall and Dunrobin to the late 1st Duke, the cost to be borne by his grieving tenantry.

Loch donated 10 guineas to each; Trentham was costed at £850. The statue is titled *Shepherd of the People* and is 3 metres tall, sitting on a column of 5 metres with a base of 2 metres, in Hollington stone. It was completed in 1836. From here at Monument Hill the whole of the 'History Tour' walk around Trentham can be viewed.

# ABOUT THE AUTHOR

Alan Myatt was born in 1945 and spent most of his life in Blurton, Staffordshire. He attended Blurton Schools and Heron Cross Secondary Modern, leaving with no qualifications. He worked as a shop assistant, brickyard worker, as a jollier on a potbank for one day, cabinetmaker at a caravan construction works, van driver and cratemaker, milkman, sewage worker and dairy worker. He eventually retrained as a television engineer, gaining City & Guild qualifications. He was made redundant after ten years and became a publican. He purchased newsagents in Pembrokeshire and Longton, sold up and became a bookselling agent until retirement in 2010. Alan has always had an interest in history and started writing local history books in 2008. He moved to Clayton when he retired. Special interests include the history of Trentham, Blurton and Longton.